BlockChain

Understanding virtual reality, Augmented, the Metaverse, NFTs, and Cryptocurrency

Koso Brown

Contents

Introduction

Imagine living in a society where you can send money to someone without the use of a bank in seconds as opposed to days and without having to pay exorbitant bank fees.

Or one where you control your money completely and store your money in an online wallet that is not connected to a bank, making you your bank. You can access it or move it without a bank's permission, and you never have to worry about a third party taking it or a government's economic policy influencing it.

This is not the world of the future; rather, it is the world in which a sizable but increasing number of early adopters currently reside. And these are just a few of the crucial blockchain technology use cases that are revolutionizing how we exchange value and build trust. The remainder will be covered later.

Yet many people still find blockchain technology to be a confusing or even frightening subject. Some people are still dubious about the potential applications of this technology. Because blockchain technology is still in its very early stages of development and wide adoption, the current level of skepticism is understandable.

What the late 1990s were to the internet, 2021 will be to the blockchain. Blockchain technology is also not a fad; it is here to stay, and if you are reading this, you are also ahead of the curve.

Chapter 1: Virtual reality (VR)

A simulated 3D environment called virtual reality allows users to explore and interact with a virtual environment in a way that simulates reality as it is experienced by the users' senses. Although the environment is created using computer hardware and software, users may also need to put on accessories like helmets or goggles to interact with it. Users are better able to suspend disbelief and treat a VR environment as real, even if it is fantastical, the more fully they can immerse themselves in it and block out their physical surroundings.

What are the various categories of virtual reality?

The VR industry still has a long way to go before achieving its goal of creating a fully immersive setting that allows users to experience a variety of sensations in a manner that is close to reality. However, the technology has advanced significantly in terms of delivering a realistic sensory experience and holds promise for commercial application in several industries.

Depending on their purpose and the technology employed, VR systems can vary greatly from one to the next, but they typically fall into one of the following three categories:

- **Non-immersive:** Typically, a 3D simulated environment that can be accessed through a computer screen is what is meant by this kind of VR. Depending on the program, the environment might also produce sound. Using a keyboard, mouse, or other devices, the user can influence the virtual environment to some extent, but the environment does not communicate with the user directly. Non-immersive VR is exemplified by video games and websites that let users customize the look of a room.

- **Semi-immersive:** This kind of VR provides a limited virtual experience that can be accessed via a computer screen, some kind of glasses, or a headset. It does not include physical movement in the same way that full immersion does and focuses primarily on the visual 3D aspect of virtual reality. The flight simulator is a typical example of semi-immersive VR and is used by both airlines and militaries to train their pilots.

- **Fully immersive:** The user has completely submerged in the virtual 3D world thanks to this type of VR, which offers the highest level of virtual reality. It includes hearing, seeing, and occasionally touching. Even some experiments with the addition of smell have been conducted. Users can fully interact with their surroundings when they are wearing specialized gear like helmets, goggles, or gloves. To give users the feeling of moving through the 3D space, the environment may also include items like treadmills or stationary bicycles. Although fully immersive VR technology is still in its infancy, it has already had a significant impact on the gaming and, to a lesser extent, the healthcare industries, and it is sparking a lot of interest across a variety of other industries.

Augmented reality

Is occasionally referred to as a subset of virtual reality, although many would contest this and say it is a different but connected field. In augmented reality, virtual simulations are superimposed on actual environments to improve or augment them. For instance, a furniture retailer might offer a mobile app that lets customers use their phones to point at a space and see what a new chair or table might look like there.

A different category that is occasionally regarded as a subset of virtual reality is mixed reality, which combines the real and virtual worlds into a single setting. Similar to augmented reality, it is more frequently viewed as a distinct but related field. It's become increasingly common to refer to virtual reality, augmented reality, and mixed reality collectively as "extended reality," which offers a convenient way to refer to all three while still differentiating them.

Numerous businesses and industry professionals are pushing for more advanced uses of the metaverse as a result of current VR technologies and applications.

How can virtual reality be used?

Because the gaming industry has been at the forefront of the VR effort and because of the success of products like Beat Saber, Minecraft VR, and Skyrim VR, virtual reality is frequently associated with gaming. However, there has been an increase in curiosity about VR's potential in several other fields:

.Training. VR makes it possible to train staff members in a safe, effective, and economical manner. People in high-risk or highly specialized occupations, such as firefighters, EMTs, police officers, soldiers, surgeons, or other medical personnel, can particularly benefit from it.

- **Education:** VR provides educational institutions with new teaching and learning techniques. While retaining their interest in the subject matter, it can give students intimate access to settings that are typically inaccessible. For instance, a history teacher could use virtual reality to take students back in time to ancient China or Greece.

- **Healthcare:** Patients, healthcare professionals, and researchers could all gain from VR in the field of healthcare. VR, for instance, has the potential to treat conditions like anorexia, anxiety, or post-traumatic stress disorder (PTSD). However, when working with patients to explain diagnoses or treatment options, doctors may be able to use VR. People with certain physical limitations may also benefit from VR.

- **Retail:** Although VR has already had some success in the retail sector, there is still much room for growth. Customers will be able to try on clothes, decorate their homes, experiment with hairstyles, test eyeglasses, and generally make better decisions about goods and services with the help of the right apps.

- **Real estate:** VR has many advantages for the real estate industry. For instance, building engineers can virtually tour HVAC systems, homeowners can see what their remodels would look like, and architects can display detailed plans in 3D.

- **Entertainment:** Although VR has already had an impact on gaming, it also holds the potential to completely change the film and television industries by giving viewers an immersive experience that immerses them in the action. Virtual reality (VR) has the potential to create a whole industry dedicated to tourism, allowing people to visit places they might never be able to visit in person.

The most basic type of virtual reality is a 3D image that can be interactively explored through a personal computer. Typically, this involves using the mouse or keyboard to move or zoom in and out of the image's content. More advanced efforts use strategies like wraparound display screens, wearable device-enhanced physical spaces, or haptic devices that allow users to "feel" the virtual images.

Chapter 2: Explaining the Metaverse

What exactly is the metaverse, though? Indeed, you can interact with what is essentially a different universe in the metaverse. But the fact that there are numerous ways to engage with the metaverse is part of what makes it so special.

With the aid of virtual reality (VR) technology, you can view the metaverse in place of your real-world perspective. While augmented reality (AR) overlays the offline world with the metaverse.

There are additional ways to interact with the metaverse. It can be accessed by everything, including mobile apps, computers, and gaming consoles. The metaverse is wholly immersive because of the ongoing overlap between the two universes. By doing so, the physical world's limitations are lifted, revealing a brand-new, limitless reality.

Your social life is included in this reality. You don't need to enter the metaverse by yourself. There are always new people to meet there, and friends and family are welcome to visit alone.

The history of the metaverse is remarkable. The metaverse's potential is exciting. It is evolving and growing continuously. Nobody can predict how the metaverse will develop because of its exponential growth.

The Earlier Version and the Metaverse's Early Days

A metaverse guide should include a thorough history of the topic. As it is currently understood, the metaverse is relatively new. However, earlier iterations have been around since the 2000s. The most accurate illustration of a proto-metaverse is Second Life, which had 900,000 active users in 2007.

Some of the things that are now regarded as essential components of the metaverse, like Roblox or Fortnite, first existed separately from it. These early metaverses developed into the larger metaverse we know today. It happens frequently for games to turn into metaverse elements. However, even the increasingly meta social networks like Facebook are heading in that direction.

The Metaverse's Characteristics

Determining the metaverse is similar to determining the conventional offline world. What matters more is which aspects either someone chooses to emphasize. It's challenging to give a precise definition of the metaverse due to its size. However, the metaverse will always have some characteristics.

It's a Limitless Environment

The metaverse is an infinite 3D space. It is infinitely explorable and has no beginning or end. Within their system, various implementations might have boundaries. These restrictions, however, are all arbitrary. Instead of being borders created because there isn't enough usable space, those are undeveloped areas.

There's No Centralization

The metaverse is not owned by any one person, group, or institution. Within the Metaverse, people can hold specific elements like land or NFTs. But the metaverse is decentralized in and of itself. No one can take ownership of a single location and take over the metaverse in its entirety. In essence, it is a user-controlled, decentralized system.

The Metaverse is Always on

There isn't a main point in the metaverse that can turn it off because there isn't a central location to control it. It resembles the offline world in many ways. Not every part of your town is always easily accessible. However, it's never truly "off."

It Has a Working Economy

Implementations of metaverses typically reflect the real world. The majority of people's daily lives depend on the economy in the real world. Thus, it should come as no surprise that metaverse cultures have a thriving economy. A metaverse economy is typically supported by the blockchain. This makes it possible to use cryptocurrencies and produce original goods.

The Metaverse is an Immersive World

The metaverse has a strong focus on immersion. You truly feel a part of the metaverse when you enter it. This is made possible by effective software and tools for extended reality. The outcome is a metaverse that you inhabit.

Metaverse settings are friendly and enjoyable

The majority of people would list socialization as one of their top priorities in life. Activities on metaverses have the potential to be equally social. Typically, metaverse geography functions in a similar way to physical geography. The metaverse is accessible to everyone. Additionally, this openness encourages group activities and socialization.

The 7 Layers of the Metaverse Serve as its foundation

You are familiar with the features of the metaverse. Additionally, Jon Radoff established seven crucial ideas that are recognized as the layers of the metaverse. These are comparable to the earth's crust, mantle, outer core, and inner core.

The 7 layers might not always be noticed by users. But when you log in, they essentially serve as your digital foundation. A thorough analysis of these seven layers can be found in Jon Radoff's "The Metaverse Value-Chain." But by reading the following summaries, you can gain a firm understanding.

1. **The Dismaterialization Experience:** The metaverse is more than just looking out into a 3D space. Dematerialization reveals the metaverse's true nature. Without requiring physical surfaces, it converts everything you know about the real world into raw data. For instance, text strings

from a book can be digitally preserved. and spatial representations of material reality. Any of these things could be represented by simulated materials in the metaverse. But in essence, they are all dematerialized items.

2. **The Excitement of Exploration and Discovery:** It is beneficial for both individuals and businesses to make discoveries. Exploring 3D spaces can lead to discovery in the metaverse. But it also refers to the overall process of content exploration. This includes products or services produced by the public and private sectors. This discovery might be outbound, with different marketers informing users via broadcast. Or it could be inbound, where a person is actively looking for details about the products and services.

3. **A Foundation for the Economy Built on the Creator Economy:** The most recent metaverse content creation tools are found in the creator economy layer. Previously, coding and design knowledge were prerequisites for creating digital spaces. But this layer's creator economy describes a way for people to quickly create and earn money from content for the metaverse. Metaverse implementations that offer specialized in-system tools frequently help with this. All of this implies that making and selling metaverse goods is simple for everyone.

4. **Boundaries are removed by spatial computing:** Spatial computing describes how the metaverse and the offline world coexist. Elements from the offline world may be made available online. Alternatively, online systems may integrate with aspects of the offline world. One of the most visible examples of this

convergence is the internet of things. It connects and digitizes everyday objects in our lives. Another example is augmented reality. AR uses locational data to visually merge the metaverse and offline worlds.

5. **Decentralization ensures that there is no single owner of the digital world:** The decentralization layer emphasizes the fact that no single entity owns the metaverse. It is better understood as a larger collective of individual components. Some of the components may be owned by a corporation. Others are owned by private individuals. And, thanks to computer assistance, blockchains make collective ownership and decision-making even more accessible. Nobody owns the entire metaverse. Because there is no single owner, no one can turn off the metaverse.

6. **The Ultimate Computer Interface Device is Humanity:** This layer explains how humanity is evolving into a computer interface device. This is largely due to wearable technology and ultraportable devices such as smartphones. Technology is shrinking, sensors are improving, and voice interfaces have become commonplace. VR goggles are becoming lighter and less reliant on external hardware. Humans can now converse with computers more naturally than ever before. And this phenomenon is becoming more advanced by the day.

7. **Everything is possible because of a strong infrastructure:** The infrastructure layer is the technology that creates and powers metaverse networks. The increasing efficiency of cellular data networks is one of the most critical aspects of this. High-speed portable Internet connections are already a reality thanks to 5G. And, eventually, 6G networks will reduce latency

while increasing speed even more. Furthermore, new engineering techniques improve the efficiency of portable electronics. Even the batteries that power mobile devices are getting better.

Chapter 3: Examples of Metaverse Usage

A metaverse guide must demonstrate both theory and application. You've seen the various elements and layers that comprise the modern metaverse. But how do these concepts take shape? The following examples highlight some of the metaverse's most important applications.

Social Media & Virtual Worlds

Virtual worlds are large 3D computer-simulated environments. Virtual worlds are essentially digital recreations of the real world. This is usually what people think of when they first hear about the metaverse.

Virtual worlds allow you to explore vast environments. You can modify your appearance by modifying the avatar that represents you. You can even engage in the same type of socialization that you would find in the real world. One of the best examples is Horizon Worlds. Meta, formerly Facebook, was created as an entirely virtual world. It's so comprehensive that people have created games within it.

Corporate

More and more businesses are going online. COVID-19 compelled many businesses to experiment with virtual meetings and workspaces for the first time. As a result, both leadership and employees discovered that they preferred the virtual model. With its Horizon Workrooms system, Meta is a pioneer in this new phenomenon.

For decades, Microsoft has been a market leader in productivity and teleconferencing systems. It's no surprise, then, that they've entered the corporate metaverse with Mesh for Microsoft Teams. Mesh's ability to leverage existing infrastructure into the metaverse space is particularly impressive.

Gaming

In many ways, gaming is the metaverse's past, present, and future. Many older online games have evolved into full-fledged metaverse experiences. Some of the best examples are Roblox, Sandbox, and Fortnite.

The metaverse's adaptability lends itself to games. When users have complete control over their environment, they frequently create their games. One of the best examples of this phenomenon is Roblox. However, platforms such as Second Life and Horizon demonstrate that people will create games with scripting and an open world. As players go online to play with their friends, gaming elements help metaverse implementations grow.

Real Estate

The scope of metaverse real estate transactions may surprise you. The metaverse's expansive 3D worlds are brimming with potential. And a virtual real estate market has sprung up in its wake. A plot of virtual land in Decentraland, for example, recently sold for USD 2.4 million. However, the existence of real estate deals in the metaverse is almost a given.

Even pro-metaverses like Second Life had a slew of large real estate transactions. Cryptocurrency and the blockchain metaverse have made modern digital real estate transactions even more accessible.

Companies Developing Metaverse Foundational Elements

The metaverse is frequently framed through the eyes of those who use it. Because the system operates on a creator-based economy, users are frequently the primary content creators. However, several businesses are also assisting in the advancement of the metaverse. These are some of the most important companies involved in the metaverse.

1. Microsoft

Microsoft places a strong emphasis on the business side of the metaverse. Microsoft has long been the industry standard for productivity software. However, it received a massive public opinion vote on the metaverse during the early days of covid-19 during the work-from-home trend.

The market for new solutions was obvious, and Microsoft released Mesh for Teams as a way to supplement their current offerings with a metaverse-based model. Mesh for Teams provides users with an avatar that they can use to explore virtual environments and workplaces. It essentially creates a perfect office environment that is accessible from anywhere.

2. Roblox

Roblox is the name of both the company and its most popular product. Roblox began as a game developer. However, the platform evolved into a far more socially and economically rich world than the creators could have imagined. This rapid expansion resulted in a fully

3D world in which users can create visually distinct avatars, clothing, and entire games that can be shared with others. Roblox is always developing new features.

One of the most significant additions is a spatial voice chat that simulates how conversations work in real life. It is also developing new clothing options.

3. Meta

Facebook has a long history of using technology to connect people. The company is certain that the metaverse is the next step in officially rebranding as Meta. Meta is working on VR hardware by creating the Oculus and the more experimental Project Cambria. Meta is also working on metaverse-based systems with Horizon. The Horizon system is constantly evolving and adding new features. This includes a marketplace and even games.

4. Niantic

Niantic is a household name in the world of augmented reality. With Pokémon GO, they brought this side of the metaverse to people's attention. This augmented reality game combined the metaverse and the offline world in an innovative way that got people off their couches and explored the virtual and physical worlds at the same time.

Niantic has raised $300 million to build a "real-world metaverse" today. Niantic CEO John Hanke describes it as "reality made better". He goes on to say that their contribution to the metaverse will be a real-world metaverse rich in data and interactive creations.

5. Nvidia

Nvidia's hardware is a critical component of the metaverse. The company investigates and develops a wide range of equipment for rendering or working with 3D graphics. They are, however, expanding into the metaverse's software side. The company recently announced a free version of its Omniverse software for digital artists.

For corporate clients, the license fee is $9,000 per year. Individual artists, on the other hand, will use it for free to experiment with the metaverse. This offer provides a valuable entry point for digital artists interested in learning more about the metaverse.

Other Organizations Working on the Metaverse

Because of the metaverse's immense potential, there is a great deal of corporate interest. Because the metaverse is essentially infinite and borderless, there is no limit to the number of companies that can collaborate with it. Google, for example, established new research divisions to collaborate with it. And industry experts are keeping a close eye on companies like Apple, which has hinted at plans.

The number of metaverse businesses is constantly increasing. In the article "Metaverse Companies Building The Future; An Overview," you can learn even more about the diverse companies developing the metaverse.

Chapter 4: The Metaverse's Formative Devices

This metaverse guide has investigated various aspects of what is available in the metaverse. But what about the devices that use it? There are several ways to access the metaverse. However, the majority of metaverse technologies fall into one of the following categories listed below.

1. Game Console

Many metaverse manifestations began as video games. As a result, it's not surprising that gaming consoles can be used to access the metaverse. Sony, in particular, is well known for its support of virtual reality. Users can use PlayStation VR headsets. And Sony has dabbled in completely social virtual environments. Even the Xbox 360, which does not have VR accessories, has some metaverse options. Users, for example, can gain access to Roblox.

2. Computers

Computers have long been at the forefront of the metaverse. Most other metaverse hardware will almost always be supported by a PC. For example, most VR hardware can be used with a PC. It is usually a matter of upgrading your computer to provide the necessary level of support. VR support, for example, typically necessitates a more powerful graphics processing unit (GPU). Thankfully, adding new hardware is relatively simple these days. The same holds for software.

3. Mobile

Mobile device metaverse support typically lags behind that of PCs and game consoles. However, advancements in cellular data and GPUs have made smartphones a more appealing platform for accessing the metaverse over time. Many VR headsets have options for pairing with smartphones. And platforms like Google Cardboard make it simple to create low-cost VR. AR games such as Pokémon GO are also popular on mobile platforms. However, leading metaverses such as Roblox support mobile.

4. Headset for Virtual Reality (VR)

Virtual reality headsets are the most well-known examples of metaverse hardware. They're fairly large headsets with a digital display that covers the user's eyes. The headset tracks the user's line of sight and constantly updates it within the metaverse software. The resolution and screen quality of a VR metaverse experience usually go hand in hand. The better the display for each eye, the more immersive it is.

5. Gear for Augmented Reality (AR)

Augmented reality allows you to see specific elements placed in the metaverse, such as AI entities or items. Augmented reality technology superimposes the metaverse on top of the real world. It typically employs a lightweight but wearable headset or smart glasses.

However, when paired with the right app, mobile devices can be considered augmented reality gear in some situations. Furthermore, some augmented reality devices connect to smartphones to provide GPS data and processing power.

A More In-Depth Look at Metaverse Devices

The most important categories have been examined in this metaverse guide. However, keep in mind that each category is only a broad overview of metaverse technology. Each category contains multiple implementations. Finding the ideal metaverse experience entails investigating what each device excels at.

Some Important Examples of Metaverse Brands

The most visible corporate element of the metaverse is hardware and software companies. They are, however, only a first step toward a larger goal. Eventually, the metaverse will have as many, if not more, business opportunities as the physical world. The following brands have crossed over from the physical world into the metaverse.

Nike Provides a Metaverse-Based Perspective on Athletics

Nike is a well-known athletic brand around the world. However, the company is also attempting to establish itself as one of the most well-known brands in the metaverse. Nike's most recent venture is a collaboration with Roblox that focuses on active lifestyles. Nickel is a project that allows users to buy Nike-branded digital goods.

Nickeland allows users to participate in a wide range of sports activities. This includes running tracks, obstacle courses, and even parks. However, Nikeland also allows people to be active while wearing it. It gives you a taste of Nike's way of life.

Vans enter the Metaverse

Vans is one of the most well-known action sports brands in the world. And, similar to Nike, they're bringing that spirit to Roblox. The company is working to make it possible for people to buy Vans products online and use them in the same way they would in the physical world.

Consider the case of someone who is a serious skater. Vans could be used in his offline practice. And he'd want to do the same thing online. Vans enabled this by making many of its products available within Roblox. They even built virtual skateparks in the metaverse to practice moves.

Gucci is High Fashion in Several Fields.

Gucci represents high fashion. For over a century, it has been associated with innovative and high-quality designs. And the corporation commemorated the occasion in the metaverse. Within Roblox, they created a stunning virtual garden exhibition.

Gucci took advantage of the opportunity to sell several unique virtual goods within the metaverse. The merchandise was only available for a limited time. Because of their rarity as digital goods, their value skyrocketed. Surprisingly, the digital version of Gucci's items has sold for more than the offline goods on which they were based.

Burberry Is Concentrating on Metaversal Honor

Burberry is a world-renowned fashion house. But they're also establishing a solid reputation in the metaverse. This is largely due to a partnership with the Honor of King's game designers. The honor of Kings featured some of Burberry's fashion lines. This includes everything from single items like coats to entire outfits.

Conclusion

One unique aspect of this marketing strategy is that items are available in both the metaverse and the real world. Someone who discovers a great Burberry look in the metaverse can replicate it in the offline world as well.